The MÄRCHEN CYCLE

Bruce McClelland

Station Hill Press

1980

Acknowledgement

Some of these poems appeared in *Text* magazine, edited by Mark Karlins, whom I thank for permssion to reprint.

Titles calligraphy by Bruce McClelland.

Frontispiece and illustration for *"The Goose Girl"* by Pam Black.

Cover illustration: Woodcut from Hartmann Schedel's *Liber Chrinicarum Mundi*, Nuremberg, 1493.
Illustration for *"Beauty & the Beast"*: Shot 144 from 'La Belle et la Bete' (1945), a film by Jean Cocteau.
Illustration for *"The Three Languages"*: "Position of the tongue for [s] and for [ʃ]." (after Hedegüs).
Illustration for *"Red"*: by Thomas Bewick. From *A New Year's Gift for Little Masters and Misses*, 1777.

Published by Station Hill Press in Barrytown, New York 12507.

Produced at the Open Studio Print Shop (187 East Market Street, Rhinebeck, N.Y.), a non-profit facility for writers, artists, & independent literary publishers, supported in part by grants from the New York State Council on the Arts & the National Endowment for the Arts.

The author would like to thank the staff of Open Studio for their valuable assistance in the production of this book.

Library of Congress Cataloging in Publication Data

McClelland, Bruce
    The Märchen cycle.

      1.   Tales, European—Poetry.   I. Title.
      PS3563.A26128M3   811'.54   80-10183
      ISBN 0-930794-26-5
      ISBN 0-930794-25-7 pbk.

CONTENTS

List of Illustrations

for mcb

"The raven is black and crucified"

The MÄRCHEN CYCLE

What are these, then,
that we should hear
so long the greybeard's
grey grows greyer, & the boy becomes
his men? These lessons,
oldman syntactic, that address us
by the spirit, if not myths, then
märchen? Diminutive,
tales of enormous instruction,
for all the psychology of them
the facts are facts. The shadow
is a moral problem, the raven
is black & crucified & the nails
fall out of his
story, his thirst
was the truth & is
no more. What can that,
just that, mean
to a curious swineherd
except he will marry
a sister of his, he's
the part she's after, & ever after
means
just that. Listen

& not hear, the story
tells itself & of itself & of a land
upon a time when
sublimation *is* transformation
& *"graybeard & boy belong together."*
& boy & girl, they, too, to
figure out the need
of the father in mother,
hear all that spontaneity,
perhaps joy, perhaps just
not, this time,
how to feel such anger
& be done. The boy will
always marry the girl
as she would him
if the old man says so
then so. Amen, the prayer
for partial wholeness
partly answered, but still
is riding hood confused
not about the teeth
themselves
               but the effect
they could have
in future stories
relating wolves

to animus. & all of us
hope for her
just to get out, alive
after all of it, not listen
but learn what to do
in the face of her own
contradiction,
these stories are *not* therapies
but ways
to become a child without
becoming. & as they are
becoming to us, let us
hear.

"Hands held the light."

Beauty & the Beast
(after Cocteau)

Then there is that father's
gold, or was
upon a time,
before & after me, ship's
riches who never came in,
in time
to see me in this
mirror, my
concern: Lost way
in lost light, to take
narrative *from* him,
& be the beast. & her & her
sisters, too, to wonder
who they'd be
in this, if not
mine. & mine
is in the movement, not
the rose itself,
the snap
           the story. (as all
good tales begin again,
this   forest where
the father finds himself

having to get lost,
loses sight of the light
that lost him here,
where the story begins,
the moment of
remembrance, to have a
daughter, & no son
ask only for the rose.
(& the story takes up with
ONLY, as if the least request,
to understand
the petals.)
        & so she does, I do,
remove it, count it
ONLY as beauty
would want it.

& I am this beast
who would take her
from that, conflict, poor &
lost old man, not lust
but memory. To accept the act
of remembering, beauty,
daughter. What was it like
to have it, something,
long lost & found
in the yield?

                    (So the trade is made,
I give myself up for him,
knowing of nothing
to lose, save the
understanding, grief.
& at seven come
to me & see my readiness, I am not,
what is ugly in this world
is still ugly to me, is that so hard
to understand?

& then the mirror, wherein
Elsewhere is
Memory, grief
at the grief
of my father
who would never know
me, away from that
mirror, in whom
I would look to see
the self, saw **ONLY**
Psyche's sisters
redeemed by the hideous,
hope, & looked again:
a glass shattered
by the intensity of
                    its reflection of

the possibilities for
beauty. & in a mirror
                          no longer
my sisters
had nothing to say.

But hands held the light,
on his face
was grief, a promise
not so much broken as
kept, the key
no longer in the key
but the magnifiicent
horse every girl
my age dreams
to ride, love for
that animal's
magnificent & the glove
the other ikon.

So beauty came to beauty
on a big white horse,
not as always, but as
a father wants it
for her, gentle
nightmare, where
the scream that wakes us
is joy.

Snow White & Rose Red

for Amy

Snow white is
Rose red, for this
night, fire lit & smoke
pulled out by
wind, the bear
that would talk &
do no harm, hammers at
the winter's door,
not to scare   but warm
him by the girls.
The one, her sister,
would feel the fur
& wonder
who would need a fire
to be between.

& it is the mother
tells these two
no father in the story,
wants this comfort,
bear by the fire. Her
winter long gone,
a year   every year
rosetrees, daughters,

this   a bear. Not a man, but
talks kindly & plays
with the girls.
& they play back,
rough   as he wants them
to remember that.

when spring comes
to the story, & he leaves
because the earth is
soft again or wet
& the dwarfs can get his
treasure from him,
he must *protect*
what he does

Which is be
a King's son
& his brother,
will be enough
for them, the complexity
of ingratitude
too much. Three times
save the dwarf, envy
the tiny balls & cock
& cut them off, his own good
is in doing nothing

to them, gives them
nothing
they haven't earned
by kindness.

But the bear,
gentle bear
who speaks & has gold on
under his fur,
his killing to become
the act itself,
hear his manly voice
& go with him,
snows white & a
roses red.

"Where she bribed the knacker"

The Goose Girl

(for Cindy)

"Take these, or this:
three red drops, white of the
handkerchief, let them
be the story
of how
they fall into the river,
& trouble begins—
begins with
         the trouble with
the story
      is
the father's long ago death
has nothing to do with it,
long ago promise
the horse will talk
if you cut off his head, the trouble is
to get around
to being sent on such a journey
& wanting to."

But goes, when she
reaches that age
the mother will give her

blood from her own
finger, points
to the white of her
cunt, then out the door. Into that
world you wanted so much
of, its husbands
to keep on with their dying
& leave you not even
a prick   for your finger,
take your drops of blood
out there & never listen
to them. & take her with you,
this maid, to teach you
who you are.
So armed with less
than advice, they go,
the fairer on Falada
who can speak, even sing
the *syllables* of his name,
Roland's Valentin, the drops
drip from the rend
in the heart. The horse
sees all
& waits to be dead
to say it: she
allowed her experience

to happen, the
teacher teaching her
to learn from such invasion,
when it happens for real
the time will have come.
To say who she is,
this princess, powerless
without the lost blood
or at least the notice
of the loss, must give
horse & voice to the maid
who made her drink of the river
with her hands,
not touch
the cup. & for this
she is to tend the geese.
(who also have nothing to do
with it but give her
something to do, a way
thru the portal
where she bribed the knacker
to hang the horse's head.)
who talks.
in her rhyme,
Orpheus hearing

the time ahead of him
when his skull will sing,
fa la da
lets her in on it,
disappointment in her
& out, Conrad
wants a snatch
of that golden hair
(matches the cup), do something
says the horse
against him. What
you will. Her will
is what she does,
no goose from that
goose boy, only a prince
to touch this stuff,
real gold, but who
can I tell it?

The good king
allows himself to hear it,
her details of who she has become
& who she is
to, the words
thru the hearth
& to his ear &

to his son, the good
never done by her mother's
blood,
but no bad. What
was heard from the horse's
mouth misunderstood
as not her own voice
& the promise is filld.
The autonomy comes
from no marriage to a prince
but what happens
to the maid.

The Fisherman & His Wife

It is a short
poem, the progress
of the sea & what

God is

is this flounder,
see, the fisher
(man) lets him

go because
he talks (the
*pro*gress
of the sea, wine
dark to

       dark-grey,
Homer talks some

same gods) only

his wife can't see

the possibilities
of leaving Him
off the hook
& winds up

as god.

Jack

the giant
slept. His own voice
pleased him more,
proved him
equal to the thief,
& falls
from that judgment:
Hurry, ma, & save me,
I've got his harp,

his heart.

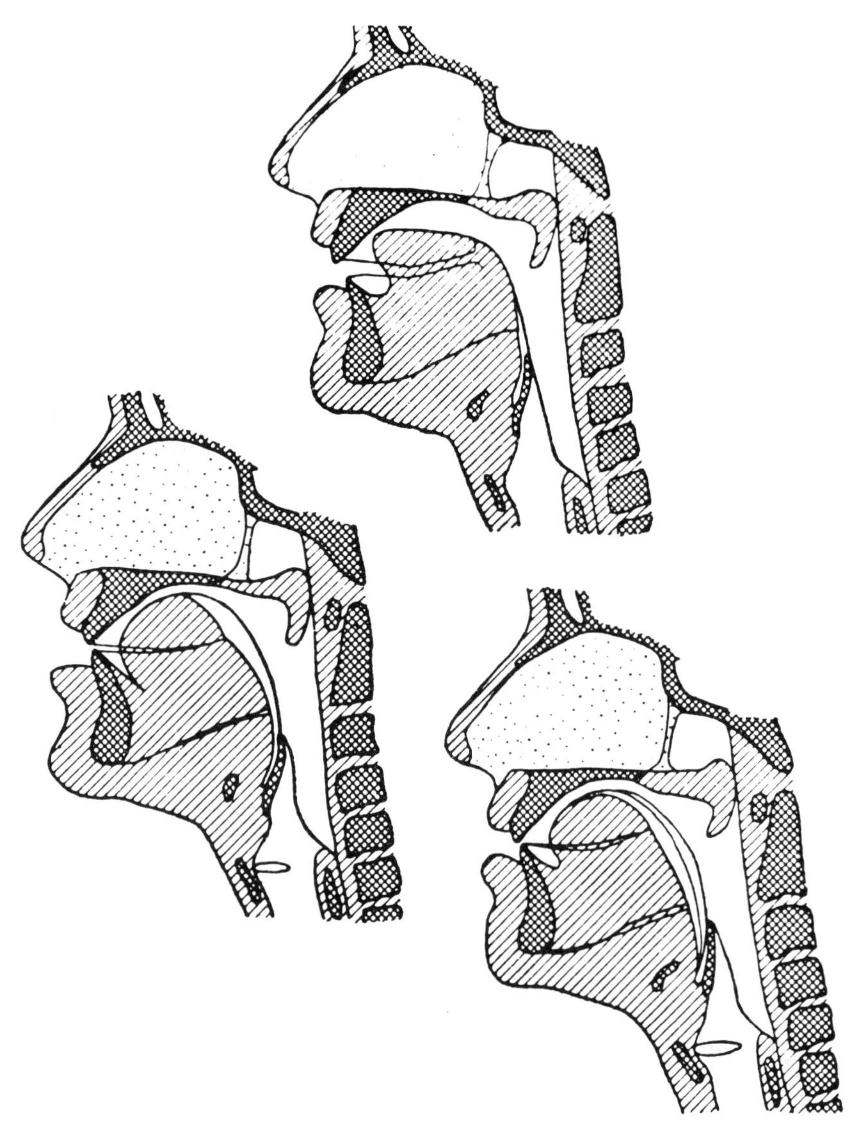

"Wild Dog, Bird, Bullfrog"

The Three Languages

There are three languages
we know of: wild dog,
bird, bullfrog. That order
comes in, & religion begins
where the wizard
or greybeard loses his son
to ancestry, loss of first
tongue
      of the deer
tells him when to rain.
         *

A year stands for time
spent listening, or not
talking back, what the wolves
might say could have been
important so the son
takes it back to the father
he learned exactly that,
useful language is
if you don't speak it.
Not song, but usefulness.
Not magic, but music.

A year wasted says
his eyes.

*

& wasted another
with some birds
who could talk
like birds, or more accurately
doves, pigeons, a coo
imitable, articulate,
involving organs
of speech & below that,
generation. To woo or lull
the masses, would need such
language, one on each
shoulder, to teach him when
to say yes
& not
say no.

He was learning
he wasn't smart, would be
Pope before his father
ever would who talked
like men, & thought
of the time he'd wasted
thinking

of the time wasted
by his son, in two full
years understood
dogs & birds, & gave him
his last chance.

Before expulsion.
If you don't come back
knowing something
there is to know or we
can talk about, son, don't
come back at all.

*

Didn't. at the end
of year three couldn't talk
to his father, the animals
had had no Word
for beginning, Religion was
unfounded, or magic was not
understood. No ground
zero for the man
to man, heart to heart,
no place to talk.
& be men, it was about,
the first language was thunder
the wizard spoke.

23

"Red"

Red

Snow now covered them,
what she saw   that road
to take her   time   to her, thyme
grew by the way it must have been
summer then
or spring or early
fall to notice, she left her house
alone to know a
way
        to take her time
on. Red said green were
the things around her
that wolf saw her wanting
to notice, summer
savory, so it must have
been, a long day's
dawdle, there, no
hurry.

(that membrane old
Biddy passed thru
one way, who wants
to get *there?*
                She didn't, pretended

it was summer, & if birds
sing, wolves talk.

Urge. Wolves hurry toward
consummation
no consecration save the
getting of
There first. Red saw it
in his eyes, not that he was certain,
death, but desire
was first thrust
at the old. No
discrimination.

No easiness
to him as a figure, speech—
bearing dilemma walking on
hinders & polite as can be.
(not what he was
but could be
his problem   hurry
up & take your time, she
drew no confusions from this.)

Time was well spent
that summer picking
pretty things
to die on her way to

the Body of
the old lady, lost sense
of the sexual, smell,
quincunxes
of youth's constellate
memory, my daughter
how vague you are

or is it me? (Have
brought something to eat,
to wake or put back
to sleep I wear
this old nightgown
because it smells like
me & I know where I am.
Is that you   I thought
would take her time
& ripen in the
is it summer

sun? It's me, said Wolf,
& if I can talk, I am
who you think.

*

It was really winter
& no one knew it
was a story about

seasons
         & Red
finding her way
thru them, from mother
to something else, a change
in timbre from inside
as she knocked, winter
pansies in the other hand,
she heard only
vagueness, smelled
wolf & sausages
in some later
water, boiled for revenge,
& entered, came in,
to it, him, & knew where
she'd come.

Machandelboom

Afraid to tell it:
tall tree & how it comes
to be, the mother she
could see a son
in snow, where no
one else's blood
could be so red
to mean
Child, she understood her body
broken by that prick,
the menstrual flew
away from her, she understands
herself as ground,
& takes the months
she needs
        the tree
            stands
offers the purple
unto, until the boy
feels her move, labor
is her death, *so freude
dat se stürw. Ehr mann*
buries her
beneath his mind, under

his need, for her, Woman, this other,
mother brings her daughter
with her, to him, & the story
is what happens
to her: her
rivalry with the poet
in the boy, the redness
of his real mother's suffering
is his face & the white
is the snow. *De Böse,*
bogey, Evil One arrives
at the mind of Step
mother & they deprive him
of his head
& do no harm. The appel
still in the hand
& the head held
(loosely) to the body
by the handkerchief
or at least the wound hid.
From her, hears nothing
from her brother
                    she wants
to, she does,
knocks his block off, the apple
& his skull roll away

together, the body topples,
there is no blood
but Marleenken
screams anyway.
Her small voice
a consecration, she hardly knows
her father
to eat that fast,
where is my boy
momma
as if I didn't know
what you put in this,
wat smeckt my dat Äten schöön,
my son, he says,
is mine, & leaves
the bones. Marleenken takes them up
again, pretends a
motherhood, she hears the
hööge Boom in de Oren,
as loud as her mother
hears *de Böses* laugh
& takes her brother's bones
to his mothers
to heal. The tree
engenders him, as bird,
& from the fire

31

to sing his self
& his story, two languages
to anyone who hears:
"My mother, who killed me
(was she the one
who heard me sing before
I was this
bird? & where is she,
that she became a tree
& what can I say
of such becoming?
That I became
my father (he) ate me
all up that I felt
wanted
to be this bird, my sister
Marlinchen
was the clever one
who gathered all the bones
in the family
of me, she tied them
in a silken handkerchief,
the texture alone
was hers, bone & silk,
silk covers bone
         bone breaks scissors

cut silk, she had me by the
bones, laid them beneath
the juniper tree
& waited
to become. There was an
anger in my beauty,
my song
was so simple   I made them pay
to hear again:
Ky-whit, ky-whit,
I in my voice
am the possibility
from treachery
& love, the recipe
for me
is all you've heard
& a piece
is all you get,
if gold fits my father's neck
& red for Marlinchen,
& I'll keep my mother
quiet.

THERE IS A CLARITY TO MYTH

that is got at
                  by its
self & without
understanding. The repetition
makes it so, the
hearing it &
the saying it
make it
moreso, clear.

In a conversation with myself
it was I
who was talking to me,
& with no insistence
on clarity, a certain myth
appeared or rather
came, as puzzle, & I
told me how
I didn't get it,
even yet,
& it was **how** I didn't get it
that I was told or
didn't get, more than
why not. & so why not
I asked, don't you get it,

with all your
lifelong understandings
of complexities, confusions,
creations of the will
against the world?
Word? I said, a question
mark. & so I said it is not always
*DIA*lectic, there is so much   we
(& that I didn't understand)
don't understand. & so this myth,
I think, that
that centers around
the Cupid & the Psyche & the fact
that that was the myth.
I pulled it in as a
ghost, or gift, to me, I said,
"look at that & looked at it,"
those being
my exact words, these,
"there it is" &
"what don't you get?"
what don't I get I said
is a good question,
ambiguous, so I took that
as having
another or two

meaning, meanings.
So I took that
as at least **HAVING**
in the sense that we own our lives
MEANING, meaning that
we own our lives
by living
right thru them,
the way
the sun can live
thru anything
that's clear.

There is this myth, then,
of those lovers,
& it is not the light
that is not understood
or loved, but only
its presence
within the room
I said
turn out that light
I said
turn out that light
& perhaps didn't have to
so I didn't
understand.

Chris Mass

Alone of all her
he was a father this
fathermas,
       send him
away, her
sex ex-
       posed to her
ex he the (true)
father saw closure
as divorcement, stars
around her as the
god dominate some
Psyche in her,
to open **THAT**
to the world:
a hero with
problem, or
No problem to evidence
itself against her lack
of what He lacked.
To open that
his desire, *ma domina*
contracted in pure
Capricorn air, stiff

goat prick stuck in there
forever until
we come to air
or her
center: magma inter-
rupts the mass,
her name Mary
Barleycorn, from Capri,
on the father's tongue
as he divides her
with spirit
from soul, a new
worold, wer eld, word
evolves as animals
asleep
wake,
          a strange
& hairless
beast born
of no name, no way
to become anything
but what he is:
the mass
from the matter,
iced fire moving through
THIS SIGN &

conquering space.
As the world
is moved into
by her parts, always giving
birth, placenta flowing
from round virgin onto
flat earth moved around
by sun until
her son becomes
a center. She wanted
that, for him:
a problem, to stick out
from his aramaic toga
when he was old enough
to know his father. His father
was long
gone when he was born
to this, but left
a branch of the tree—
of the soul of man,
astronomy, to three men
to be counted on
to gossip
about the way of the world
they were headed & followed
their own proboscis

to this narrative
of simplicity. An answer
to the previous
answer   was to give
the gods
no sex among themselves,
simplify. This god
would have gender by virtue
of name & nothing
else. His mother
would still be
the earth   but the magma
would cool & become
thicket where no man
could want to wander
who was man.

But man wanders,
the god himself
coldens, the animals
sleep or walk away,
missa est, event ex-
perienced, the mass is
said.

The text was phototypeset by the author in 14 point Century Old Style, and printed at the Open Studio Print Shop in Rhinebeck, New York. This first edition was designed by the author, and is limited to 1200 copies, of which 43 have been signed and numbered.